CONTENTS

G000292898

Introduction
Foreword
Top Tips .... page 5

STARTERS
Sa-tay Chicken & Sa-tay King Prawns .... page 6
Fish Cakes .... page 9
Fresh Spring Rolls (V) .... page 10
Crispy Spring Rolls with Crabmeat .... page 13
Sweetcorn Cakes (V) .... page 14

SOUPS
Dr. Atique's Hot Toddy (V) .... page 15
Tom Yum (V) .... page 16
Yum Yum Special Soup (V) .... page 19
Tom Khar (V) .... page 20

SALADS
Yum Nok - hot & sour salad with grilled guinea fowl .... page 21
Som Tam - spicy green papaya salad (V) .... page 22
Yum Neau - grilled beef salad with chilli, onions and lime juice ...... page 25
Lab To-fu - spicy to-fu salad with mushrooms and Thai herbs (V) ...... page 26
Yum Tuna - spicy tuna salad .... page 29

THAI CURRIES
Curry Pastes .... page 30
Mussaman Curry Paste .... page 32
Kang Kiew Wan Kai - green curry with chicken, coconut milk, Thai aubergines and Thai herbs ...... page 35
Kang Ped Phed - special red curry with roast duck ...... page 36
Kang Mussaman - lamb peanut butter curry .... page 39
Kang Gaeng - yellow curry with pumpkin and to-fu (V) ...... page 40
Kang Pla - orange curry with monkfish .... page 43

CONTENTS

MAIN DISHES
Ped Ma Kam - crispy roast duck with tamarind sauce   page 44
Lok Kai Yum Yum- roast baby chicken with red wine sauce   page 47
Moo-yang Pad Bo - marinated pork with stir-fried crabmeat, ginger and spring onion   page 48
Pla Neung Prik-Thai Onn - steamed sea bass with green peppercorns and special soy sauce page 51
Pla Sam Rod - deep-fried fish with chef's special sauce   page 52
Goong Pad Prik-king - king prawns with chilli and green beans   page 55
Murk Prew-wan - sweet & sour squid with tomato, pineapple and cucumber   page 56

RICE, NOODLES, EGGS & VEGETABLES
Pad Thai - traditional Thai fried noodles   page 59
Pad Thai Jay - traditional Thai fried noodles (V)   page 59
Pad Se-iew - stir-fried Thai rice noodles with vegetables, egg and dark soy sauce (V)   page 60
Khao Soy - steamed noodles with fresh beancurd (V) or chicken   page 63
Kai Tiaow - Thai-style omelette (V)   page 64
Kao Pad Pised - special fried rice with chicken and prawns   page 65
Coconut Rice (V)   page 65
Pad Pak Kom - quick-fried spinach with garlic and yellow beans (V)   page 66
Pad Ma-khea - sautéed aubergines (V)   page 69

DESSERTS
Hot Chocolate Fondant (V)   page 70
Lemongrass Crème Brûlée (V)   page 73
Lime & Coconut Cheesecake (V)   page 74

COCKTAILS
Introduction and Grant's Shaking Tips   page 76
YumYum's Mojito   page 79
Red Snapper   page 80
Bangkok Breakfast   page 83
Heavy Weight   page 84
Spring Summer (non-alcoholic)   page 87
Abstinence on the Beach (non-alcoholic)   page 87

Dipping Sauces   page 88
Where to find it - a guide to sourcing Thai ingredients   page 90
Acknowledgments   page 91

INTRODUCTION

It's almost thirteen years since we began serving classic Thai cuisine in Stoke Newington. When we started out in Church Street all that time ago, we never imagined that we would one day be serving over a thousand diners a week in a grand eighteenth century listed building around the corner. Yet thanks to our loyal friends and customers, at the time of writing we are now celebrating our first anniversary in our fabulous new home. To mark this special occasion we are proud to introduce to you our very own cookbook, signifying yet another important milestone in the history of YumYum.

On the following pages you'll learn the secrets behind your favourite YumYum dishes, so you can impress friends, lovers and family alike with a sumptuous Thai feast created in the comfort of your own home. You'll also find a few recipes that don't currently appear on our restaurant menu, just to spice things up even more!

All the recipes have been thoroughly put through their paces in the home kitchen and we hope you find them easy to follow. You'll also find plenty of tips, including where to source some of those hard-to-locate Thai ingredients.

We wish you good luck in your new journey of exploration into Thai cooking and hope you enjoy using our book as much as we enjoy running the restaurant.

Don't forget to come over for a meal and tell us how you're getting on!

From all of us at YumYum

FOREWORD

I'm delighted to welcome you to the YumYum Cookbook and hope you'll find plenty in it to enjoy.

In Thailand, the essence of every meal is harmony, aiming for an overall balance of tastes and textures, with careful thought being given to the four principal Thai tastes – spicy hot, sour, sweet and salty.

Our recipes are not set in stone, so be adventurous and try out variations, such as adding herbs and spices in different proportions, to suit your palate; or introducing a few additional ingredients you particularly like.

Thai people have a big reputation for picking and snacking endlessly between meals, but they still seem to find room to enjoy the main family spread of the day. Unlike the western custom of serving separate courses, a number of dishes are put on the table at the same time for everyone to share. So why not bring real authenticity to your Thai experiments by serving up a soup, a salad, a curry and a stir-fry all at once, accompanied of course by rice or noodles, and followed by a dessert of fresh exotic fruits.

Another significant difference between Thai cuisine and that of western Europe is that virtually everything consumed in Thailand comes from local sources. This raises for us the topical issues of air miles and eco-responsibility. We live in a modern world where there are no boundaries to tastes, cuisines, or the foods we can obtain. A green curry can be made with ostrich or kangaroo farmed in Berkshire, and kaffir lime leaves can be ordered from nurseries in Sussex. Equally, however, New Zealand mussels can be bought as readily as the plump, juicy natives of North Norfolk, and shitake mushrooms from China are just as available as those grown in the Midlands. Although many ingredients in our recipes have to be imported - and there really is no way round this at present - at YumYum we are constantly striving to increase the amount of local produce we use above imported goods. We urge you to try to do the same.

Wishing you all the best.

Atique Choudhury

TOP TIPS

- Woks should be heated dry before adding oil or any other ingredients.

- Curries improve with slow-cooking over a period of time to allow the flavours to mature. The longer you leave them, the better they will taste.

- Make salads as spicy hot as possible and, if you like, include exotic fruits.

- Vegetables should be stir-fried briefly in a thin oriental wok to retain their crispness, colour and goodness.

- Invest in a rice cooker. In the Thai home, rice is kept in the cooker throughout the day and remains in perfect condition.

IMPORTANT NOTES

- Metric weights and measures have been used throughout.

- Teaspoons and tablespoons of ingredients should be level unless otherwise stated.

- There are variations in the number of people each recipe will serve. In our restaurant each dish is cooked to order and is usually for one portion. Take care to note the quantities given in the recipes and adjust accordingly where necessary.

- We have not included information about preparation times as cooks' abilities vary a great deal: some will chop an onion in seconds whilst others may take several times longer. But a quick glance through a recipe should give a good indication of how much time is needed for the dish to be cooked once the ingredients are prepared.

SA-TAY CHICKEN & SA-TAY KING PRAWNS

barbecued or grilled chicken & king prawns marinated in Thai herbs

PER PERSON: I skinless chicken breast fillet, bashed with a tenderiser or rolling pin to flatten slightly, then cut lengthways into three or four strips, or 3-4 jumbo prawns, peeled and deveined.

FOR THE MARINADE: The quantities given below are sufficient for four chicken breasts or a dozen jumbo prawns.

- I tablespoon caster sugar
- 2 teaspoons medium curry powder
- 2 teaspoons turmeric
- 2 teaspoons sea salt
- 2 teaspoons ground white pepper
- I tablespoon thick oyster sauce
- I tin coconut milk: ¾ tin for the marinade, the remainder for basting during cooking
- 4 kaffir lime leaves, thinly sliced
- 8 sweet basil leaves, shredded or torn
- 2 tablespoons extra virgin olive oil

- I8cm/7" bamboo skewers, previously soaked in water to prevent burning

GARNISH: Lime wedges, mixed salad leaves
TO SERVE: Peanut dipping sauce

1. Place all the marinade ingredients in a large bowl and stir thoroughly.
2. Add the chicken strips or prawns, making sure they are all well coated.
3. Cover the bowl with clingfilm and leave in the fridge for I-2 hours.
4. Using tongs, pick the chicken or prawns piece by piece from the marinade, shaking to remove excess liquid, then thread them onto the skewers. When this has been completed, the marinade can be discarded.
5. Whilst threading, pre-heat grill or griddle to medium hot, or have your barbecue ready for cooking.
6. Cook the chicken or prawns for 2 minutes, turn skewers over and brush with coconut milk.
7. Cook for 2 minutes more, turn and brush again.
8. Repeat, so that there will have been a total of 8 minutes' cooking time.
9. Arrange the garnish on a large platter, or, if you prefer, divide between individual plates, and place the sa-tay skewers on top.

FISH CAKES

A permanent fixture on the menu, our ever-popular fish cakes are fantastic finger food for parties. Quick and easy to make, they are equally delicious hot, warm, or at room temperature. As part of a buffet or as a starter, allow 3-4 cakes per person.

FOR APPROXIMATELY 20-24 CAKES:
- 250g skinless cod fillet or mixed white fish
- 80g king prawns, shelled but uncooked
- 2 medium eggs
- 2 teaspoons red curry paste
- 2 teaspoons salt
- 30g cornflour
- 30g long beans or French beans, finely sliced (optional)
- 4 kaffir lime leaves, finely sliced
- 1 litre corn or vegetable oil for deep frying
- Plain flour for dusting tray

GARNISH:
- Lime wedges, coriander leaves
TO SERVE:
- Plum and sweet chilli dipping sauces, carrot & cucumber relish

1. In a food processor, mince the fish for 10 seconds, then add the prawns and whizz for another 10 seconds.
2. Break the eggs into the processor, add the curry paste and salt, and blend with the fish for 20 seconds. Tip in the cornflour, and blend for another 20 seconds or so until the consistency is quite thick and gooey.
3. Spoon the mixture into a large bowl and stir in the beans and lime leaves.
4. Take a teaspoonful of the mixture per cake, using both hands, shape into small patties of about 3 cm diameter and 1 cm deep. Have a bowl of water at the ready and periodically moisten your hands.
5. Put the shaped cakes on a lightly floured tray and chill in the fridge for an hour or so.
6. Heat the oil in the wok. When the oil just begins to smoke, lift the cakes individually using a fish slice and drop them into the oil.
7. Fry in batches of 6-8 at a time for about 2 minutes on each side, until golden brown.
8. Remove with a slotted spoon and drain on kitchen paper. The cakes should be quite springy when pressed. If they are not, drop them back in the hot oil for a minute longer.
9. Arrange on a platter, decorate with the lime wedges and sprinklings of coriander leaves, and serve the sauces separately in small bowls.

FRESH SPRING ROLLS

These healthy rolls combine rice pancakes with crunchy salad and herbs. The pancakes can be found in many oriental stores in packets of 12. You can, of course, vary the filling as much as you like. Try adding cooked sliced prawn, julienned spring onion or finely sliced red onion.

PER PERSON:
- 4 oriental rice pancakes
- Handful of cooked vermicelli noodles
- ½ a cucumber, julienned
- ½ a medium carrot, julienned
- Handful of mint leaves, chopped
- Handful of coriander leaves, chopped
- 2-3 leaves iceberg lettuce, shredded

TO SERVE:
- Chilli dipping sauce

The best way to go about things is to be labour-intensive: make the complete rolls one by one and cover the finished articles with a clean damp tea towel to prevent them drying out.

1. Begin by mixing the vermicelli, vegetables and herbs together in a bowl.
2. Soak a pancake in hot water for half a minute, then place it on a clean, dry tea towel and pat to remove excess moisture.
3. Spoon a quarter of the mix into the centre of the pancake.
4. Bring the left and right flaps of the pancake into the centre, over the mix, so they overlap slightly and stick together.
5. From the bottom, gently roll up the pancake as tightly as possible and press to stick.
6. Repeat with all the other pancakes.
7. Arrange on individual plates or on a platter and serve the sauce separately.

CRISPY SPRING ROLLS WITH CRABMEAT

MAKES 2 WHOLE ROLLS/FOUR HALVES:
- 2 crabsticks, shredded
- 100g mixed minced boneless chicken breast and minced prawn, both uncooked
- 1 tablespoon cornflour
- 1 teaspoon salt
- 1 tablespoon sesame oil
- 1 medium egg, white and yolk separated
- 1 heaped teaspoon diced carrot
- 1 spring onion, sliced
- 2 spring roll pastry squares.
- 2 x 1cm wide strips Japanese nori seaweed
- 1 litre corn or vegetable oil for deep frying

TO SERVE:
- Plum dipping sauce

1. Combine the chicken and prawn with the crabstick meat, stir in the cornflour, salt and sesame oil, then mix in the egg white, carrot and spring onion.
2. Place spring roll squares on worktop in a diamond-shaped configuration, so their corners face north, south, east and west.
3. Spoon the mix in horizontal lines just below centre and roll up, beginning south to north. When the mix has been enclosed, bring east and west corners to meet in the middle then continue rolling south to north.
4. Using a dab of beaten egg yolk, attach a seaweed strip to each north corner and wrap around the whole spring roll.
5. Join the seaweed together using more egg yolk.
6. Heat the oil in a deep pan or wok.
7. Cook the rolls for about five minutes, or until they rise to the surface.
8. Drain on kitchen paper before serving.
9. Slice rolls in half if wished.

SWEETCORN CAKES

These savoury vegetarian cakes are great fun for kids to make because of the gooeyness of the cake mixture. It goes without saying that an adult should take over when it's time to cook them.

A vegetarian red curry paste recipe can be found in the Pastes chapter (page 30). As with many curry pastes, if you are buying it in a jar from a shop, do check for the presence of shrimp.

TO MAKE APPROXIMATELY 24 CAKES:
- 1 large (330g) tin plain sweetcorn, drained
- 2 tablespoons peas, cooked from frozen, refreshed under cold water and drained
- 2 medium eggs
- 2 teaspoons red curry paste
- 2 teaspoons salt
- 1 teaspoon ground white pepper
- 2 tablespoons cornflour
- 2 tablespoons self-raising flour
- 2 tablespoons plain flour, plus extra for flouring chopping board
- 1 litre corn or vegetable oil for deep frying

TO SERVE:
- Sweet chilli dipping sauce

1. Empty the sweetcorn into a large mixing bowl, add the peas and break in the eggs.
2. Stir in the curry paste, salt, pepper and flours, and combine thoroughly until you have a dense mixture that becomes quite resistant to stirring.
3. Lightly flour a chopping board.
4. Take a dessertspoonful of the mixture at a time and shape into little cakes using your hands. It helps if you also have a bowl of water ready and wet your hands periodically.
5. Lay the cakes out on the chopping board.
6. Heat the wok and add the oil. When oil looks medium hot, test whether it is ready by dropping in a single cake and seeing how quickly this puffs up and rises to the surface. It is important that the oil is not too hot, or the sweetcorn will burn.
7. Using a fish slice, transfer the cakes to the wok, 6-8 at a time.
8. Deep fry for approximately half a minute per batch, turning frequently with a slotted spoon, until golden brown.
9. Drain on kitchen paper, and arrange on individual plates or a large platter. Serve the sauce separately.

DR. ATIQUE'S HOT TODDY

or, "how I fix my friends"

This daring version of Tom Yum works like a fiery magic potion and is a natural remedy for coughs, colds and sore throats. For maximum impact you should boil the stock with the chillies for a couple of minutes, then leave to cool and infuse for 24 hours before continuing with the recipe.

SERVES 2:
- 300ml chicken or vegetable stock.
- 3 red birdseye chillies, finely sliced, with seeds retained
- 6 slices galangal – about 3cm length in all
- 6 slices lemongrass, cut diagonally in 1cm lengths from bulbous end
- 2 kaffir lime leaves, roughly torn, centre stalk discarded if wished
- 6 grinds of the black pepper mill
- 6 oyster mushrooms, sliced
- 2 teaspoons fish or soy sauce (depending on whether you want non-vegetarian or vegetarian soup)
- One lime, halved
- 10-15 coriander leaves, picked off the stalk

1. Make up the stock and bring to the boil in a saucepan or wok.
2. Drop in the chillies, lemongrass, galangal and lime leaves, and add the black pepper.
3. Boil for half a minute, then reduce to a simmer.
4. Add the mushrooms.
5. Continue simmering for 3-4 minutes, then stir in the fish or soy sauce.
6. Remove from heat and ladle into bowls.
7. Squeeze the juice of half a lime over each bowl and stir.
8. Sprinkle some coriander leaves on top.

Take your time sipping the liquid. Its effects should be noticeable instantly!

TOM YUM

The classic spicy-hot clear broth, Tom Yum is one of the two essential Thai soup bases and can be added to with vegetarian or non-vegetarian extras. Below the basic recipe you will find some of the variations which appear on our menu.

SERVES 2:
- 300ml chicken or vegetable stock
- 6 slices peeled galangal – about 3cm length in all
- 6 slices lemongrass, cut diagonally in 1cm lengths
- 2 kaffir lime leaves, centre stalk discarded if wished, roughly torn
- 1 red birdseye chilli, finely sliced, with seeds retained if wished
- 4-6 oyster mushrooms, sliced
- 2 tablespoons fish or soy sauce (depending on whether you want non-vegetarian or vegetarian soup)
- One lime, halved

GARNISH:
- 10 coriander leaves

1. Make up the stock and bring to the boil in a saucepan or wok.
2. Drop in the lemongrass, galangal, lime leaves and chilli.
3. Boil for half a minute, then reduce to a simmer.
4. Add the mushrooms and any extra ingredients you have chosen.
5. Simmer for 3-4 minutes, then add the fish or soy sauce.
6. Check that any extra ingredients are cooked through: prawns should have turned pink, whilst chicken should have no hint of pink.
7. Ladle into two bowls, squeeze the juice of half a lime over each bowl and stir.
8. Add a sprinkling of coriander leaves.

TOM YUM KAI:
Add 4-6 thin slices skinless chicken breast
TOM YUM GOONG:
Add 4-6 shelled raw king prawns
TOM YUM SEAFOOD:
Add 50g or so mixed seafood, such as mussels, prawns and squid, together with a couple of extra lemongrass slices.
TOM YUM VEGETARIAN:
Add 50g sliced shitake or clear mushrooms, and an extra torn lime leaf.

YUM YUM SPECIAL SOUP

This is a real feelgood soup. Filling, nutritious, and a comforting winter warmer, it can be ready in just ten minutes.

SERVES 2
VEGETARIAN VERSION:
- 300ml vegetable stock
- 4 chunks deep-fried to-fu, sliced
- 2 tablespoons diced carrot
- 2 tablespoons frozen peas
- 2 large shitake mushrooms, diced
- 2 large oyster mushrooms, halved, two of the halves then diced
- 2 tablespoons chopped spring onion
- 2 tablespoons light soy sauce
- 2 tablespoons lemon juice
- 2 teaspoons cornflour, mixed with a little cold water
- 2 medium eggs, whisked

1. Heat the stock in a wok or saucepan.
2. When bubbling, add all the vegetables and bring to the boil.
3. Reduce heat a little, add the soy sauce and lemon juice, stir in the cornflour and continue stirring until the stock thickens.
4. Pour in the egg mixture and agitate quickly with a fork or a whisk, as if you were making scrambled egg.
5. When the egg white becomes opaque the soup is ready.

NON-VEGETARIAN VERSION:
1. Take two slices of skinless chicken breast, finely chopped or minced, and two peeled, deveined king prawns which may be chopped or left whole.
2. Follow the recipe above and add these to the stock when the vegetables go in. Chicken stock may be substituted for the vegetable stock, if wished.

TOM KHAR

The second essential soup base, Tom Khar is characterised by the inclusion of coconut milk, creating a sweet, rich taste.

Follow the recipe for Tom Yum (page 16) but make the following alterations:

- 175ml chicken or vegetable stock and 175ml coconut milk instead of 300ml stock.
- Add the coconut milk when the stock begins to boil.
- Use 1 teaspoon fish or soy sauce instead of 2.

As with Tom Yum, add seafood, chicken, mushrooms or vegetables as desired.

YUM NOK
hot & sour salad with grilled guinea fowl

This delicate-looking salad has real kick when combined with its sharp dressing, and there are many additions that will complement it beautifully. Citrus-glazed guinea fowl is a suggested accompaniment, but you could also be wildly extravagant by adding slices of cooked lobster, a handful of crayfish tails and a couple of langoustines instead, and vegetarians might like to try it with chargrilled white asparagus.

PER PERSON:
- Coriander – 20 whole leaves
- Mint – 20 whole leaves
- 2 spring onions, finely sliced lengthways
- ½ a medium red onion, peeled and finely sliced
- 2 long red chillies, deseeded and finely sliced lengthways
- ¼ of a red pepper, deseeded and finely sliced
- Handful of salad leaves, torn, or mixed baby leaves. Escarole and frisée work well

Simply combine all the above ingredients in a salad bowl. Pour over the dressing just before serving and toss well.

FOR THE DRESSING (100ml - enough for 2 servings):
- Juice of 4 limes
- 2 tablespoons fish sauce
- ½ level teaspoon hot chilli powder
- 2 teaspoons sirop de gomme or sugar syrup

GRILLED CITRUS GUINEA FOWL:
- I guinea fowl breast
- I tablespoon clementine marmalade
- I tablespoon lime marmalade
- 2 teaspoons hoisin sauce

1. Combine the marmalades and sauce in a pan and heat gently until melted. Stir.
2. Preheat the grill to medium hot.
3. Brush the guinea fowl with the sauce and grill until the juices run clear when pricked with a fork. Baste frequently with more sauce to prevent the meat becoming too dry.
4. Allow to rest whilst you make the salad and dressing, then slice into five or six pieces on the diagonal. Add the guinea fowl to the salad, pour over the dressing, and toss thoroughly.

SOM TAM
spicy green papaya salad

A Thai version of coleslaw, this crunchy salad combines cooling green papaya with a ferocious dressing and can be put together very quickly using a food processor. If time is on your side, however, try doing it the old-fashioned way by grating the papaya with a mandoline and using a pestle and mortar to make the dressing: it really does make all the difference.

SERVES 2:
- 50g palm sugar
- 2 red birdseye chillies
- 4 cloves garlic, peeled
- 4 tablespoons freshly-squeezed lime juice
- 2 tablespoons fish or soy sauce
- 8 cherry tomatoes, halved
- ½ a green papaya, peeled and grated – about 200g
- 1 medium carrot, peeled and grated
- 3 Thai long beans or 6 French beans, topped and tailed and each cut into 4 pieces
- 2 tablespoons roasted peanuts, crushed

1. Place the palm sugar in a plastic container and soften in the microwave on full power for 10 seconds.
2. Pound the whole chillies with the garlic, then add the palm sugar, which will begin to dissolve.
3. Stir in the lime juice and the fish or soy sauce, followed by the cherry tomatoes.
4. Pound again briefly.
5. Place the papaya, carrots and beans in a mixing bowl, sprinkle the crushed peanuts over, then pour on the dressing.
6. Mix thoroughly to coat everything with the dressing.

YUM NEAU
grilled beef salad with chilli, onions and lime juice

SERVES 2 AS A STARTER OR ONE AS A
MAIN COURSE:
- 1 sirloin or fillet steak
- Salt, black pepper
- Corn or vegetable oil for brushing steak
- 1 red birdseye chilli, seeds retained, sliced
  on the diagonal
- 1 teaspoon chilli sauce
- 1 tablespoon fish sauce
- 1 tablespoon freshly-squeezed lime juice
- 1 red onion, thinly sliced
- ½ a stick of celery, de-stringed and sliced
- ½ a medium carrot, peeled, and julienned
  or grated
- 3 cherry tomatoes, halved
- Small handful of mint leaves, torn

TO SERVE:
- ½ a cucumber, cut into half-moon slices.
- Mixed leaf salad

1. Lightly season the beef with salt and pepper
   and brush with oil.
2. Grill on a chargrill, barbecue or on a pre-heated
   ridged griddle plate.
3. When cooked to your liking, remove from the
   heat and allow to rest.
4. In a bowl mix together the fish and chilli
   sauces, the lime juice and the sliced red chilli.
5. In a salad bowl toss together the red onion,
   celery, carrot, cherry tomatoes and mint
   leaves.
6. Thinly slice the beef and add to the salad
   together with the sauce.
7. Toss again.
8. Arrange the mixed salad leaves and cucumber
   slices on a plate and spoon the beef salad
   into the centre in a mound.

LAB TO-FU

spicy to-fu salad with mushrooms and Thai herbs

PER PERSON:
- 200g firm to-fu (beancurd), drained and cut into 4-6 chunks
- 2 large oyster mushrooms, sliced
- ½ a medium carrot, finely julienned
- 1 small red onion, finely chopped
- 1 spring onion, sliced into thin rounds

FOR THE DRESSING:
- 1 heaped tablespoon of Thai jasmine rice (for the rice powder see 1 & 2 opposite)
- Juice of one lime
- ½ teaspoon dried crushed red chillies
- 1 teaspoon caster sugar
- 2 teaspoons fish or soy sauce
- Small handful of coriander leaves
- Small handful of mint leaves
- Corn or vegetable oil for deep frying

Begin by making the rice powder.

1. Place the rice in a saucepan and heat, dry, until it begins to turn golden brown.
2. Remove from heat, let the rice cool, then finely grind in a spice grinder. Only a teaspoonful is required in this recipe, so keep the remainder in a small airtight container for future use.
3. Make the dressing in a large bowl by adding 1 teaspoon rice powder to all the other dressing ingredients. Stir well.
4. Heat the wok, add the oil and, when medium hot, fry the to-fu until golden brown.
5. Add the oyster mushrooms and continue frying until the mushrooms are crispy.
6. Remove to-fu and mushrooms from wok with a slotted spoon and drain on kitchen paper.
7. Mix the salad ingredients and herbs together in the bowl containing the dressing.
8. Roughly chop the to-fu and mushrooms, add to bowl and combine throughly.
9. Garnish with the herbs.

YUM TUNA
spicy tuna salad

PER PERSON:
- I fresh tuna steak
- I tablespoon chilli oil
- ½ a medium red onion, finely chopped
- I red birdseye chilli, deseeded and sliced
- I green birdseye chilli, deseeded and sliced
- I long red chilli, deseeded and finely sliced lengthways
- ½ a stick of lemongrass, bulbous end, finely sliced on the diagonal
- I spring onion, finely sliced lengthways
- 10-15 coriander leaves, picked from the stalk and roughly chopped
- 2 cloves garlic, crushed
- Salt and pepper to taste

FOR THE DRESSING:
- Juice of 2 limes
- 2 tablespoons fish sauce
- ¼ teaspoon hot chilli powder
- I teaspoon caster sugar
- 2 tablespoons tamarind water

OPTIONAL EXTRA:
- A handful of dried shrimp, soaked for 10 minutes then sautéed in a little oil until crisp and crunchy.

1. Pre-heat grill or griddle.
2. Brush the tuna on both sides with the chilli oil, and cook for 2-3 minutes each side, or until just cooked through but slightly pink in the centre. The addition of lime juice later will 'cook' the tuna a little more.
3. Allow to cool, then transfer to a bowl and flake or mash the tuna.
3. Mix in all the other ingredients and shrimp if using.
4. Make up the dressing in a separate bowl or jug and pour half onto the salad, mixing throughly.

If you like, accompany with traditional Salade Niçoise ingredients: salted tomatoes, red and green peppers, broad beans or French beans, spring onions - all sliced, chopped or cut as you wish. Pour the remainder of the dressing over these. As to the egg element of this French classic, quarters of hardboiled salted duck egg instead of hen's egg would add an extra dimension but is something of an acquired taste. The choice is yours!

CURRY PASTES

The ingredients lists on jars or tubs of commercial curry pastes will reveal that there are dozens of variations, some more elaborate than others. Beyond the absolute essentials – green chillies for a green paste, turmeric for a yellow paste and so forth - it is almost a matter of personal taste: some like it hot, others like it hotter. Unless you're in a rush and need to resort to off-the-shelf brands, do try making your own as you'll find homemade pastes taste far superior.

All of these basic recipes are vegetarian but you can, of course, add a couple of teaspoons of roasted shrimp paste if wished. If you like testing your patience, try blending the ingredients using a pestle and mortar. Otherwise, a good electric blender - preferably with four blades rather than two - is your best friend. These versions will take 5-10 minutes to make using a blender. Whichever method you choose, begin with the driest ingredients. If the going gets tough, as it often does - especially with fibrous lemongrass - adding around 25ml of water should make things easier. When you blend the pastes mechanically, periodically take off the lid of the goblet to mix up and push down the ingredients. The pastes will keep in airtight containers in the fridge for up to a week or can be frozen.

CURRY PASTES

GREEN CURRY PASTE
- 2 red shallots, peeled and halved
- 5 coriander roots, cleaned and roughly chopped
- 3 green birdseye chillies, seeds retained
- 1 piece peeled galangal, about 30g, sliced
- 1 stick lemongrass, sliced
- 3 kaffir lime leaves, torn

RED CURRY PASTE
- 1 tablespoon soya oil
- 3 red birdseye chillies, seeds retained
- 1 piece peeled galangal, about 30g, sliced
- 2 teaspoons freshly-squeezed lime juice
- 6 kaffir lime leaves, torn
- 1 stick lemongrass, sliced
- 1 teaspoon caster sugar
- 1 teaspoon salt

YELLOW CURRY PASTE
- ½ a red onion, chopped
- 4 cloves garlic, about 10g, chopped
- 1 piece peeled galangal, about 30g, sliced
- 20 dried red birdseye chillies, soaked in warm water for 10 minutes, then drained. This makes the paste blindingly hot. (Use half the quantity of chillies if nervous, or deseed the chillies before soaking.)
- 2 heaped teaspoons yellow turmeric powder
- 1 teaspoon white peppercorns
- 1 teaspoon salt

MUSSAMAN CURRY PASTE

Definitely not a quickie. Make it on a dull weekend when you have an hour or two to spare. The aroma of the roasting spices will send the spirits soaring.

FOR THE BASIC PASTE:
- 1 medium red onion, peeled and chopped
- 6 medium cloves garlic, peeled and halved
- Bulbous half of a stick of lemongrass, finely sliced
- 5 coriander roots, cleaned and chopped
- 5cm piece galangal, peeled and sliced
- 10 long dried red chillies, deseeded, soaked in warm water for 10 minutes, then drained

FOR THE SPICE POWDER:
- 1½ teaspoons coriander seeds
- 2 cardamom pods
- 1 teaspoon cumin seeds
- 2cm piece cassia bark, or a few smaller pieces
- 1 star anise, broken up
- 3 cloves
- ½ teaspoon ground mace
- 1 tablespoon sea salt
- 2 tablespoons dry-roasted peanuts

First make the paste.
1. Heat the wok without any oil or water and put in the onion, garlic, lemongrass, coriander root and galangal. Dry-roast gently for about 10 minutes or until the ingredients have softened and browned. Keep everything moving around the wok to prevent burning.
2. Remove from wok and leave to cool, then transfer to the blender and add the chillies. Blend to a paste then leave in the blender whilst you make the spice powder. Wipe the cooled wok with kitchen paper.
3. Combine all the spices in a mixing bowl and add a little water – about 2 tablespoons – to moisten them. Heat the wok to medium and dry-roast the spices for about 10 minutes, stirring occasionally, until you can really smell the fragrance.
4. Turn off the heat, remove the spices from the wok, place in a spice/coffee grinder and grind to a powder.
5. Transfer the powder to the blender and add the sea salt.
6. Wipe out the grinder and add the peanuts, grind quite finely, then add the peanuts to the blender.
7. Blend for 10 seconds and the paste is ready for use.

KANG KIEW WAN KAI

green curry with chicken, coconut milk, Thai aubergines and Thai herbs

Green curry will go happily with king prawns or mixed vegetables instead of chicken. Kra chai is not absolutely essential but adds a delicate peppery gingerness to the curry, and if you cannot obtain round green Thai aubergines use chunks of regular aubergine instead.

SERVES 2:
- 2 heaped teaspoons green curry paste (see page 31)
- 2 tablespoons corn or vegetable oil
- 1 tin coconut milk, stirred
- 1 skinless chicken breast, cut into thin slices
- 250ml chicken stock
- 2 tablespoons fish sauce
- 2 heaped tablespoons bamboo shoots
- 4 heaped teaspoons shredded kra chai
- 2 Thai aubergines, quartered
- 1 courgette, quartered lengthways on the diagonal
- Handful of sweet basil leaves, shredded
- 2 kaffir lime leaves, halved
- ½ a green pepper, sliced
- 2 tablespoons extra virgin olive oil – as green as you can find

1. Heat the wok moderately, add the oil and the the curry paste and fry gently for a minute.
2. Mix in 2 tablespoons of the coconut milk and cook for half a minute, stirring continuously.
3. Add the chicken slices and continue cooking, still stirring, for 2 minutes more.
4. Pour in the rest of the coconut milk, followed by the chicken stock, and stir again.
5. Bring up to the boil, then reduce heat and simmer for 5 minutes.
6. Add fish sauce, bamboo shoots, kra chai, aubergines and courgette.
7. Simmer for 5 minutes more, then add sweet basil, lime leaves and green pepper.
8. Cook for a further couple of minutes.
9. Finally, stir in the olive oil.

KANG PED PHED

special red curry with roast duck

Roasted Barbary duck breasts are excellent for this recipe but, for a truly authentic taste, try ready-prepared Cantonese-style roast duck, which is available vacuum-packed from some oriental supermarkets.

SERVES 2:

- 4 teaspoons red curry paste (see page 31)
- 2 tablespoons corn or vegetable oil
- 1 tin coconut milk
- 1 small aubergine, cut into chunks
- 300ml chicken stock
- 2 teaspoons salt
- 4 teaspoons fish sauce
- 1 roasted duck breast, thinly sliced
- 12 small chunks fresh pineapple
- 100g bamboo shoots
- 2 cherry tomatoes
- 3 Thai long beans or 6 French beans, cut into thirds
- 2 kaffir lime leaves
- Handful of sweet basil leaves

1. In a heated wok, mix the red curry paste with the oil and cook gently for one minute.
2. Add half the coconut milk, then the aubergine chunks.
3. Simmer for 3-4 minutes.
4. Pour in the remainder of the coconut milk, the stock, salt and fish sauce, and continue simmering until the aubergine has completely softened – about 5 minutes.
5. Add the roast duck and all the other ingredients and stir thoroughly.
6. Cook gently for a further 5 minutes or until all the ingredients feel tender when tested with a fork.

KANG MUSSAMAN
lamb peanut butter curry

Our award-winning signature dish! We use mixed cuts of shoulder and leg of lamb, on and off the bone respectively, but you may prefer just to use boned cubed leg. We recommend using fresh Mussaman Paste (page 32) but you can also buy this in jars. Tinned pumpkin can be used if fresh cannot be found.

SERVES 2:
- 2 star anise, broken up
- 2 pieces cassia bark or cinnamon stick, about 10g, broken up
- 2 litres water
- 400g lamb (British organic for preference)
- 1 teaspoon turmeric
- 1 heaped tablespoon Mussaman curry paste
- 1 heaped tablespoon crunchy peanut butter
- 1 tin coconut milk
- 500ml lamb or chicken stock, or water
- 1 tablespoon soy sauce
- 1 teaspoon salt
- 25g palm sugar
- 2 teaspoons tamarind paste
- 1 medium-sized potato, peeles and quartered
- 150g pumpkin, cut into bite-size chunks
- 1 tablespoon corn or vegetable oil

TO GARNISH:
- 3-4 slices red pepper
- 3-4 slices green pepper
- 12 roasted cashew nuts
- 2 cherry tomatoes
- 2 whole dried red chillies

1. In a large pan or stockpot, bring the water to a rolling boil with the cassia or cinnamon bark and star anise.
2. Add the lamb and turmeric. Cook just above simmering for 15 minutes, then drain, discarding the cooking liquid.
3. Heat the wok and add the oil, then the Mussaman paste, peanut butter and half the coconut milk.
4. Simmer, stirring continuously, for a couple of minutes, then add the lamb and the stock or water, followed by the soy sauce, salt, palm sugar and tamarind paste.
5. Stir again, bring up to the boil, then leave to simmer very gently for 45 minutes.
6. Add the potato and pumpkin. Simmer for a further 15 minutes.
7. Use a fork to check that lamb, potato and pumpkin are all tender, then add the remaining coconut milk and garnish ingredients.
8. Simmer for 5 minutes more.

KANG GAENG
yellow curry with pumpkin and to-fu

SERVES 2:
- 2 teaspoons yellow curry paste (see page 31)
- 1 teaspoon turmeric
- 1 tin coconut milk
- 250ml water
- 2 teaspoons tamarind paste
- 2 teaspoons caster sugar
- 2 teaspoons salt
- 6-8 bite-size chunks pumpkin
- 2 oyster mushrooms, sliced
- 6-8 slices red, green and yellow pepper
- 10-12 cubes to-fu, deep fried until golden
- 2 tablespoons corn or vegetable oil

1. Heat the wok, add the oil, and stir in the curry paste and turmeric.
2. Cook on a medium heat for one minute.
3. Add 2 tablespoons coconut milk and stir well to amalgamate.
4. Add the water, tamarind paste, sugar and salt and cook for a further minute.
5. Add the pumpkin, reduce heat, and simmer for 10 minutes.
6. Place all the other ingredients in the wok and continuing simmering for about 5 minutes, or until pumpkin is tender when tested with a fork.

KANG PLA
orange curry with monkfish

Orange curries are thin, hot, sour and salty, uncomplicated and quick to make. We have chosen monkfish because it holds together well, but any other type of firm white fish would work equally successfully.

SERVES 2:
FOR THE TAMARIND WATER:
- Mix a teaspoon of tamarind paste with 100ml boiling water. Stir well.

FOR THE PASTE:
- 5 long (6cm) orange chillies, deseeded if wished, and chopped
- 1 tablespoon galangal, peeled and chopped
- 3 tablespoons red onion or red shallot, peeled and chopped
- 1 teaspoon salt
- 1 tablespoon tomato purée
- 2 tablespoons tamarind water

- 400g monkfish fillet, cut into thin slices
- 750ml fish stock
- 3 tablespoons tamarind water
- 3 tablespoons fish sauce
- 3 teaspoons caster sugar

- 200g mixed vegetables of your choice, all cut into manageable bite-size pieces. Suggested additions are bamboo shoots, swiss chard, rainbow chard or whole baby leaf spinach, white asparagus, tomberries if you can get them, or a few halved cherry tomatoes.

1. Make the paste in a blender (5-10 mins) and leave it there for the moment.
2. In a wok, bring the stock to the boil and drop in about a third of the monkfish.
3. Turn heat down to a simmer and cook the fish for 2 minutes.
4. Using a slotted spoon, remove the fish and put into the blender with the curry paste.
5. Blend to combine. This will give extra body to the curry.
6. Return the fish stock to the boil, then add the tamarind water, fish sauce and sugar.
7. Stir the paste from the blender into the stock.
8. Bring stock back to the boil then start adding the vegetables, beginning with those that take longest to cook. End with the more delicate vegetables such as the spinach or chard. Cook on a fast simmer for a couple of minutes.
9. Finally, add the rest of the sliced monkfish and cook on a gentle simmer for a couple more minutes or until the fish is opaque.

PED MA KAM
crispy roast duck with tamarind sauce

PER PERSON:
- 1 Barbary duck breast, rubbed with salt and pepper on both sides
- 1 tablespoon corn or vegetable oil
- 2 teaspoons sesame seeds

FOR THE SAUCE:
- 3 teaspoons tamarind paste
- 1 teaspoon hoisin sauce
- 1 teaspoon salt
- 2 teaspoons caster sugar
- 125ml water

1. Pre-heat the oven to 220° C/Gas Mark 7
2. Heat the oil in a frying pan and fry the duck for one minute on each side.
3. Transfer to the hot oven and roast on a rack in a roasting tin for 10 minutes.
4. Remove from oven and leave to rest for 5 minutes.
5. Meanwhile, in a saucepan mix together all the sauce ingredients and heat, stirring, until it bubbles and the sugar begins to caramelise.
6. After a couple of minutes the liquid will have reduced down to a thick sauce.
7. Slice the duck into half a dozen pieces and arrange on a plate, keeping the slices neatly together.
8. Pour the sauce over and sprinkle with the sesame seeds.

LOK KAI YUM YUM
roast baby chicken with red wine sauce

This popular dish looks fabulously impressive if you make it using one whole poussin per person, but is equally delicious with your choice of chicken joints – corn-fed for preference.

PER PERSON:
FOR THE SAUCE:
- 1 tablespoon hot chilli sauce
- 1 tablespoon sweet chilli sauce
- 5 tablespoons dry red wine
- 3 tablespoons tomato ketchup
- 2 tablespoons light soy sauce
- 2 teaspoons sugar

- 1 oven-ready poussin

- 1 tablespoon sesame oil
- 2-3 button mushrooms, quartered
- ½ a white onion, quartered
- 1 tablespoon diced carrot
- 2 spring onion stalks, green parts only, sliced
- 2 long dried red chillies

1. Pre-heat the oven to 200°C/Gas Mark 6
2. Make up the red wine sauce recipe by combining all the ingredients. Stir well, then pour half the sauce into another bowl, reserving the rest.
3. With a basting brush, coat the poussin with some of the sauce from one of the bowls.
4. Roast the poussin on a rack in a roasting tin in the oven for 30-40 minutes, basting every 10 minutes with the remaining sauce from the same bowl. When cooked, remove from oven and leave to rest while you stir-fry the vegetables.
5. Heat the wok, add the sesame oil and heat until medium-hot, then add the onion, carrot and mushrooms.
6. Stir-fry for a few seconds.
7. Pour the contents of the second bowl of sauce into the wok and cook for a further 2 minutes or until sauce thickens, stirring continuously.
8. Add the spring onion and dried chilli and cook for a further half minute.
9. Place the poussin on a warm plate and arrange the vegetables in red wine around it.

MOO-YANG PAD BO

marinated pork with stir-fried crabmeat, ginger and spring onion

This is a versatile recipe. If preferred you can cut the pork into strips after marinating, then stir-fry in the wok for 2-3 minutes before adding the other ingredients. You can also introduce other items to the stir-fry such as morning glory, Chinese celery, or rounds of thinly sliced lemongrass.

FOR 2 SERVINGS:
- 2 pork steaks

FOR THE MARINADE:
- 2 tablespoons sweet soy sauce (Ketjap Manis)
- 2 tablespoons fish sauce
- 2 tablespoons light soy sauce
- 1 teaspoon caster sugar
- 1 tablespoon fennel seeds, lightly crushed
- 2 garlic cloves, crushed

FOR THE STIR FRY:
- 1 tablespoon corn or vegetable oil
- 1 tablespoon toasted sesame oil
- 100g white crabmeat, defrosted if frozen
- 4 spring onions, halved then sliced again lengthways
- 5cm peeled piece root ginger, sliced lengthways into thin sticks

1. Make up the marinade in a bowl. Place pork in a shallow dish, pour the marinade over and turn pork to make sure the meat is well coated.
2. Cover the dish and leave to chill in the fridge for at least an hour.
3. Prepare the stir fry ingredients and heat the grill to medium-hot.
4. Using tongs or a slotted spoon, remove pork from the marinade and grill under a medium heat for 6-7 minutes each side, basting with more marinade as you cook to keep the meat moist.
5. Turn off the grill and leave pork there whilst you heat the wok and add the two oils.
6. When oil is medium hot, briskly stir-fry the ginger and spring onion for a minute until onion begins to wilt, add the crabmeat and continue stir-frying for half a minute.
7. Pour 4 tablespoons of the marinade into the wok and cook for a further half minute.
8. Transfer the pork to individual plates and use a slotted spoon to arrange the stir-fry ingredients equally on top of each portion.
9. Finish off by spooning the juices from the wok around the pork.

PLA NEUNG PRIK-THAI ONN

steamed sea bass with green peppercorns and special soy sauce

PER PERSON:
- 1 whole sea bass, gutted
- 1 tablespoon fresh green peppercorns
- 2 tablespoons fresh root ginger, peeled and julienned
- ½ a long red chilli, deseeded and julienned
- 1 spring onion, halved and julienned
- Handful of coriander leaves

FOR THE SAUCE:
- 125ml fish stock
- 1 tablespoon dark soy sauce or mushroom soy sauce
- 3 teaspoons medium soy sauce
- 3 teaspoons oyster sauce
- 1 teaspoon toasted sesame oil

- 2 tablespoons corn or vegetable oil

1. Bring a pan of water to the boil and reduce to a bubbling simmer.
2. Place the sea bass in a steamer or colander over the pan and cover with a lid or with foil.
3. Steam for 15 minutes or until cooked through. Alternatively, use a fish kettle, or microwave in a covered dish.
4. Meanwhile, make the sauce. Warm the fish stock in a saucepan and add the soy sauces, oyster sauce and sesame oil.
5. Transfer the fish to a serving plate.
6. Heat a wok, add the oil and when hot stir-fry the peppercorns, ginger, chilli, spring onion and coriander leaves for just 15 seconds.
7. Remove immediately with a slotted spoon.
8. Arrange the stir-fried ingredients on top of the fish, then spoon the sauce over.

PLA SAM ROD
deep fried fish with chef's special sauce

Red sea bream is ideal for this recipe but you could experiment with many other types of white fish. If deep frying doesn't appeal, you can steam, poach or bake your chosen fish.

PER PERSON:
- Tail end of ½ a sea bream
- 1 litre corn or vegetable oil for deep frying

FOR THE PASTE:
- 3 garlic cloves
- 1 long red chilli, deseeded
- 2 red birdseye chillies, deseeded
- ¾ stalk lemongrass, wider end
- 1 large lime leaf, torn
- ¼ of a small red onion
- 2 slices peeled galangal

FOR THE SAUCE:
- 2 tablespoons vegetable oil
- 2 tablespoons caster sugar
- 1 tablespoon tamarind paste
- 2 tablespoons light soy sauce
- 150ml fish stock
- 1 tablespoon cornflour, mixed with a little cold water
- Handful of sweet basil leaves
- ½ a long red chilli, sliced on the bias, seeds left in

FOR THE BATTER:
- 100g plain flour
- 2 teaspoons table salt
- 2 teaspoons ground white pepper
- 1 medium egg

1. Combine all the batter ingredients thoroughly and add sufficient water to make a liquid sticky enough to coat the fish. Leave to rest.
2. Mix the paste ingredients in a blender.
3. Heat the wok, add the oil and when warmed add the paste, soy, sugar, chilli and tamarind. Stir well, then pour in three quarters of the stock.
4. Add the cornflour to the wok ingredients, then the basil leaves and the remainder of the stock, and stir well until the liquid thickens.
5. Keep the sauce warm whilst you fry the fish.
6. Heat the oil in the deep fryer and when hot coat the fish in the batter. Lower in the fish, and cook until golden brown.
7. Transfer to a warm plate and pour the sauce over before serving.

GOONG PAD PRIK-KING

king prawns with chilli and green beans

PER PERSON:
- 6 king prawns, size 26/30 for preference, peeled and deveined
- 1 tablespoon red curry paste
- 1 teaspoon caster sugar
- 1 kaffir lime leaf, torn into quarters
- 1 long red chilli, sliced on the diagonal, seeds retained
- ½ a dozen Thai long or 1 dozen French beans, topped and tailed and sliced into thirds
- 100ml full fat milk
- 2 tablespoons corn or vegetable oil

1. Heat the wok, add the oil and when hot stir-fry the prawns until they begin to turn pink – about 30 seconds.
2. Stir in the red curry paste, followed by the sugar and lime leaf.
3. Stir again, then add the chilli and the green beans, followed by the milk.
4. Bring to bubbling point and cook, stirring continuously for about 2 minutes or until the sauce has thickened.

MURK PREW-WAN
sweet & sour squid with tomato, pineapple and cucumber

PER PERSON:
- 3-4 small prepared squid, cut into rings or pieces as wished
- ½ a dozen small chunks fresh pineapple
- 1 tomato, quartered
- ¼ of a cucumber, cut into half a dozen batons
- ¼ of a white onion, roughly chopped
- ¼ red and ¼ green pepper, sliced
- 3-4 slices carrot

FOR THE SAUCE:
- 2 tablespoons caster sugar
- 1 tablespoon white vinegar
- 1 tablespoon light soy sauce
- 1 tablespoon hot chilli sauce
- 1 tablespoon tomato ketchup

- Small bowl of cornflour
- ½ a litre corn or vegetable oil for deep frying
- 2 tablespoons corn or vegetable oil for stir-frying

1. Blend all the sauce ingredients together in a mixing bowl.
2. Coat the squid pieces in the cornflour.
3. Heat the wok, add the oil and when very hot, deep-fry the squid for one minute.
4. Remove with a slotted spoon and drain on kitchen paper.
5. Transfer the oil to a heatproof receptacle and return wok to the heat.
6. Add the 2 tablespoons oil and when hot briefly stir-fry the vegetables and fruit.
7. Pour the sauce into the wok and cook for one minute.
8. Add the fried squid, stirring to coat with the sauce.
9. Cook for 2 minutes or until the sauce has thickened.

PAD THAI & PAD THAI JAY

traditional Thai fried noodles

Pad Thai is what might be called the national noodle dish and features crispy beansprouts, spring onions, palm sugar and roasted peanuts. You can make the traditional Pad Thai with cooked prawns, shrimp or chicken; or the vegetarian version, Pad Thai Jay, by adding slices of to-fu.

SERVES 2:
- 6 tablespoons corn or vegetable oil
- 2 tablespoons red onion or shallot, chopped
- 2 tablespoons dried radish
- 1 medium carrot, peeled and julienned
- 125g medium rice noodles
- 2 tablespoons fish sauce (for Pad Thai) or light soy sauce (for Pad Thai Jay)
- 2 tablespoons tamarind paste
- 4 teaspoons caster sugar
- 2 tablespoons crushed roasted peanuts
- 4 heaped tablespoons beansprouts
- 2-4 to-fu slices, or a handful of cooked prawns, shrimp or chicken, finely diced or shredded.
- 1 teaspoon crushed dried red chilli
- 2 spring onions, halved, then julienned
- 2 medium eggs, brought to room temperature and beaten

1. Begin by preparing the noodles. Soak these in warm water for 5 minutes, then drain.
2. Heat the wok, add the oil, and when it begins to smoke put in the ingredients in the following order for the length of time given. Use a slotted spoon and keep the ingredients moving round the wok at a rapid pace.
   1. Red onion or shallot, dried radish and carrot – 10 seconds
   2. Noodles – 10 seconds
   3. Fish or soy sauce and tamarind paste – 10 seconds
   4. 1 teaspoon caster sugar – 10 seconds
   5. Crushed peanuts – 10 seconds
   6. To-fu slices if using, plus remainder of vegetables, chilli, 3 teaspoons caster sugar – 20 seconds.
3. Pour the beaten egg over the noodles and vegetables and leave the mixture to cook on its own for 10 seconds, so that it takes on the shape and appearance of an omelette.
4. Flip as you would when making pancakes, then scramble the mixture up with a pair of forks.
5. If using cooked prawns, shrimp or chicken, add at this stage and toss everything together thoroughly one last time.
6. Serve very hot, topped with extra crushed roasted peanuts if wished.

PAD SE-IEW

stir-fried Thai rice noodles with vegetables, egg and dark soy sauce

SERVES 2 :
- 4 tablespoons corn or vegetable oil
- 400g soft ribbon noodles
- 2 teaspoons dark soy sauce
- 2 teaspoons caster sugar
- 2 tablespoons light soy sauce
- 1 dozen mangetout or French beans, destringed and halved
- 1 dozen slices carrot
- ½ dozen small broccoli florets
- ½ dozen small cauliflower florets
- 2 medium eggs

1. Heat the wok, add the oil and heat up until medium hot.
2. Stir-fry the noodles for about 30 seconds, making sure they are well coated with the oil.
3. Add the dark soy, followed by the sugar and light soy, again making sure the noodles are well coated.
5. Add all the vegetables and stir-fry for 2-3 minutes: the larger the broccoli and cauliflower florets, the more time will be needed to cook them through.
6. Crack the eggs over the noodles so they land whole, as if you were frying them for breakfast.
7. As soon as the eggs begin to cook, scramble them vigorously into the noodles.
8. Serve very hot.

KHAO SOY
steamed noodles with fresh beancurd or chicken

Khao Soy – a noodle dish from the north of Thailand – is a meal in itself, and has the bonus of being very healthy. The close relationship of egg noodles to pasta is why we call this dish a Thai version of fettucine.

PER SERVING:
- 1 tablespoon corn or vegetable oil
- 1 teaspoon yellow curry paste
- ¼ tin coconut milk
- 250ml vegetable or chicken stock
- 2 tablespoons soy sauce
- 2 teaspoons caster sugar
- 4-5 cubes fresh beancurd, either uncooked or deep-fried according to preference, or 3-4 slices skinless chicken breast
- 40g ribbon egg noodles or ribbon pasta

TO GARNISH:
- 1 heaped tablespoon pickled mustard leaf or pickled white cabbage
- 1 heaped tablespoon beansprouts
- ¼ of a red onion, finely sliced
- 1 dried red chilli, crumbled
- 1 tablespoon freshly-squeezed lime juice

1. Begin by making the sauce. Heat the wok and add the oil.
2. Mix in the yellow curry paste and a little of the coconut milk to loosen the paste.
3. Stir, and cook for half a minute on a medium heat.
4. Add the stock, the remainder of the coconut milk, sugar, soy sauce and beancurd or chicken slices.
5. Simmer for 5 minutes.
6. Meanwhile, cook the noodles in a steamer placed over a pan of boiling water, for around 7 minutes. If using pasta, cook in boiling water until al dente.
7. Drain and transfer to a pasta or soup bowl, then ladle the sauce from the wok over the noodles.
8. Place the garnish ingredients on top, add the lime juice and gently toss everything together using spoons, as you would with pasta and a sauce.

KAI TIAOW
Thai-style omelette

The beauty of this dish is that it is quick and easy to prepare, and can be varied in endless ways. Below is the most basic recipe, to which you can add a couple of tablespoons of your choice of extras towards the end of cooking.

PER SERVING:
- 3 medium eggs
- 1 shallot, finely sliced
- 1-2 red birdseye chillies, halved, deseeded, then finely sliced
- 1 tablespoon chopped coriander leaves
- Greener half of a spring onion, finely sliced
- Salt and pepper to taste
- 1 tablespoon corn or vegetable oil for frying

- Extras could include a handful of beansprouts, sliced cooked mushrooms, crushed peanuts, grated carrot, dried salted radish, or a combination of these. You will need about 4 tablespoons in all.

GARNISH:
- Julienned red and green pepper, spring onion or cucumber and finely sliced chives.

ACCOMPANIMENTS:
- Sweet chilli sauce and light soy sauce.

1. Beat the eggs thoroughly in a bowl and add the shallot, chillies, coriander leaves and onion.
2. Add the seasoning.
3. Heat the wok, add the oil, and swirl it around the pan as evenly as possible.
4. When faintly smoking, add the egg mixture.
5. Swirl the mixture around the wok to make a thin omelette approx 20-24cm in diameter.
6. Continue swirling gently for a couple of minutes or until the egg mixture is almost set, then spoon across the centre any extras you wish to include.
7. Slide the omelette out onto a plate, allow to cool for a moment, then roll it up.
8. Leave for 5 minutes, then slice across as you would a roulade. The omelette will look more attractive if you slice it on the diagonal.
9. Arrange on a plate and add the garnish.

KAO PAD PISED

special fried rice with chicken and prawns

SERVES 2 AS A MAIN DISH:
- 1 tablespoon corn or vegetable oil
- 1 star anise
- 1 piece cassia bark, about 5g
- 250g cooked Thai jasmine rice
- 150g chicken breast, minced
- 50g shelled prawns, finely chopped
- 1 tablespoon red curry paste
- 2 tablespoons light soy sauce
- 2 tablespoons chopped spring onion

GARNISH:
- Cucumber slices and tomato wedges

1. Heat the wok and add the oil.
2. When hot, break in the bark and star anise.
3. Add the minced chicken and prawn and stir-fry briefly for about 10 seconds.
4. Add the curry paste and continue stir-frying for about a minute.
5. Pour in the soy sauce and stir-fry for a further 30 seconds.
6. Add the cooked rice and stir vigorously to combine.
7. Turn out into a bowl and sprinkle with the chopped spring onion.
8. Garnish with the tomato and cucumber.

COCONUT RICE

SERVES 4:
- 250g basmati rice, soaked for five minutes in cold water
- 750ml cold water
- 50g coconut milk powder (We recommend Maggi.)
- 1 teaspoon salt
- 20g caster sugar
- 1 tablespoon toasted sesame seeds

1. Wash the soaked rice thoroughly under cold running water.
2. Place in a saucepan with the 750ml water and add the coconut milk powder, sugar and salt. Stir well to combine.
3. Bring to the boil, then turn the heat down.
4. Partly cover the pan with a lid and simmer for about 15 minutes.
5. Check rice is tender and water has been absorbed.
6. Take pan off heat and leave to stand for 5 minutes. This will give the rice its sticky quality.
7. Serve sprinkled with the toasted sesame seeds.

PAD PAK KOM

quick-fried spinach with garlic and yellow beans

A perennial favourite, there is something irresistible about this juicy vegetable dish. The beans are not vital but do add colour and a deep saltiness.

SERVES 2 AS A SIDE DISH:
- 4 large cloves garlic, finely chopped
- 50ml corn or vegetable oil
- 250ml water
- 250g fresh spinach on the stalk
- I teaspoon yellow soya beans
- I tablespoon oyster or dark soy sauce
- I tablespoon light soy sauce

1. Heat the wok on medium-high, add half the oil and heat for 15 seconds.
2. Stir-fry the garlic for just 10 seconds, then remove with a slotted spoon and drain on kitchen paper.
3. Leaving the oil in the wok, add the water and bring to a rolling boil.
4. When bubbling throw in the spinach and stir-boil for 20 seconds.
5. Remove wok from heat and tip contents into a colander.
6. Drain the spinach, pressing with the back of a tablespoon to extract excess water.
7. Return wok to the heat, add remaining oil, and, when hot, stir-fry the drained spinach for 10 seconds.
8. Add oyster or dark soy sauce, light soy sauce and yellow beans.
9. Stir fry for 20 seconds more, arrange on a plate and sprinkle with the fried garlic.

PAD MA-KHEA

sautéed aubergines

SERVES 2 AS A SIDE DISH:

- ½ a regular aubergine, sliced diagonally into rounds, then each slice halved
- ¼ of a white onion, sliced
- 1 heaped tablespoon bamboo shoots
- 6 slices red and green pepper
- 1 teaspoon hot chilli sauce
- 1 tablespoon Special Sauce (see recipe for Deep Fried Fish with Chef's Special Sauce on page 52)
- Handful of sweet or holy basil leaves
- 100ml water
- 1 tablespoon light soy sauce
- 250ml corn or vegetable oil for frying

1. Heat the wok, add the oil and heat until very hot.
2. Fry the aubergines for ten seconds, stirring constantly with a slotted spoon.
3. Remove wok from heat and drain off oil, leaving the aubergines.
4. Stir in the Special Sauce, then add the onion, bamboo shoots, peppers and hot chilli sauce.
5. Stir-fry on a high heat for a minute or so, then add the water, followed by the light soy sauce and basil leaves.
6. Stir-fry for about three minutes more or until the aubergine is cooked through and is tender when tested with a fork.

HOT CHOCOLATE FONDANT

You will need 4 ramekins or dariole moulds.

SERVES 4:
- 25g unsalted butter, melted
- Cocoa powder
- 150g good quality dark chocolate, 60-70% cacao
- 150g unsalted butter, cubed
- 3 whole eggs, brought to room temperature
- 3 egg yolks, brought to room temperature
- 200g caster sugar
- 75g plain flour

1. Begin by lightly brushing 4 ramekins or dariole moulds with the melted butter. Leave these to chill in the fridge for at least half an hour, then dredge them with cocoa powder. If you don't have a dredger, use a small sieve to sift the powder onto the butter.
2. Melt the chocolate and cubed butter in a bowl over a pan of simmering water, stirring gently.
3. Beat the whole eggs in a bowl with the caster sugar.
4. Pour the egg and sugar mix onto the chocolate and butter mix and gently blend together. Add the egg yolks and continue blending.
5. Sift the flour into the mixture and lightly fold in using a whisk. It is important not to over mix at this stage.
6. Pour the mix into the ramekins or dariole moulds and chill in the fridge for 1-2 hours.
7. Preheat the oven to 180°C/Gas Mark 4 and bake the puddings for 12-14 minutes, checking after 10 minutes that the tops are not cracking. If they are, reduce the oven temperature slightly. When the centres begin to rise, the puddings are ready.
8. Carefully turn the puddings out onto warmed plates.
9. Finish by sifting a little cocoa powder around each pudding.

LEMONGRASS CRÈME BRÛLÉE

A delicious twist on the classic dessert of Burnt Cream, blending European and Asian tastes. Begin 48 hours ahead.

You will need 6 ramekins.

FOR 6 SERVINGS:
- 500ml double cream
- 8 medium egg yolks, brought to room temperature
- 125g caster sugar plus extra to sprinkle over the set cream
- 1 vanilla pod, split
- 3 stalks lemongrass

TO GARNISH:
- Julienned citrus zest

1. Begin by smashing the lemongrass stalks with a tenderiser or rolling pin.
2. Pour the cream into a bowl, add the lemongrass, cover and refrigerate for 2 days.

TO COOK:
3. Pour the cream with the lemongrass into a saucepan and bring to scalding point – just below boiling.
4. Whilst the cream is heating, beat the egg yolks with the sugar.
5. Strain the lemongrass cream onto the eggs and sugar, whisk briefly and transfer to a double boiler, adding the vanilla pod. Discard the lemongrass at this point.
6. Simmer gently until the mixture thickens into a custard - enough to adhere to the back of a wooden spoon - then strain into individual ramekins or bowls and leave to cool.
7. Chill in the fridge until set (minimum 4 hours).
8. Neatly sprinkle a light layer of caster sugar over each bowl, then either place under a pre-heated hot grill until sugar begins to bubble, caramelise and turn golden brown, or burn the sugar with a blowtorch.
9. Cool and chill again, then decorate with the lemon, lime and orange zest.

LIME & COCONUT CHEESECAKE

with a passionfruit coulis

Serves 6-10, depending on how much of a sweet tooth everyone has.

You will need an 18cm diameter springform tin.

FOR THE BISCUIT BASE:
- 100g plain digestive biscuits
- 60g unsalted butter, melted
- 40g dessicated coconut, lightly toasted under the grill

FOR THE CHEESECAKE MIXTURE:
- 300g cream cheese
- 100g mascarpone cheese
- 100g caster sugar
- 2 whole eggs and 2 egg yolks
- 1 teaspoon vanilla extract
- Grated zest and juice of 2 limes

1. Break up the biscuits roughly and place in food processor. Whizz until they have become fine crumbs.
2. Add the butter and coconut, and process again.
3. Spoon the mixture into the springform tin and press down evenly with the back of a spoon. Put into the fridge for half an hour.
4. Place the cheeses in a mixing bowl and beat until the consistency is smooth.
5. Add the sugar and beat in, then the eggs, egg yolks, vanilla extract, lime juice and grated zest. Beat again to make sure everything is well combined.
6. Heat the oven to 180°C/Gas Mark 4 and boil a litre of water.
7. Take the tin out of the fridge and double wrap with foil, so the base and sides of the tin are tightly covered.
8. Put the tin in a roasting pan and pour in enough hot water into the pan to come about halfway up the tin.
9. Pour the cheesecake mix into the tin, carefully place the pan in the oven, and leave to cook for about 50 minutes or until the top of the cheesecake feels firm to the touch. Meanwhile, if you are intending to include the topping, whisk together the topping ingredients.

LIME & COCONUT CHEESECAKE

with a passionfruit coulis

FOR THE TOPPING (OPTIONAL):
- Small tub soured cream
- 1 tablespoon caster sugar
- 2 drops vanilla extract

TO DECORATE:
- Julienned zest of 1 lime

FOR THE COULIS:
- 6 passionfruit
- 4 tablespoons caster sugar

10. Gently slide the rack containing the pan halfway out of the oven and pour the topping mixture over the cheesecake, then with equal care slide it back and continue baking for a further 10 minutes.
11. Remove the pan from the oven and – using oven gloves – take the tin out of the pan.
12. Leave the tin to cool completely on a wire rack, then remove the foil wrapping.
13. Sprinkle the julienned lime zest on the top of the cheesecake and place the cheesecake, still in the tin, in the fridge.
14. Chill for at least 2 hours.
15. To make the coulis, cut the passionfruits in half and, using a teaspoon, scoop out the juices and seeds into the food processor.
16. Whizz until the juice is frothy.
17. Strain the juice into a small saucepan, and warm through on a low heat. Discard the seeds.
18. Add the sugar to the warm juice and stir gently until dissolved. Leave to cool.
19. Take the cheesecake out of the fridge 10 minutes before you are ready to serve it.
20. Unclip the spring and slowly push the cheesecake up on its base.
21. Using a knife dipped in hot water, cut the cheesecake and transfer the slices to individual plates.
22. Finally, spoon equal quantities of the coulis onto each plate.

COCKTAILS

At YumYum we are proud to offer an unequalled range of drinks to suit all tastes, from an extensive selection of wines carefully chosen to complement our dishes to a vast array of premium spirits, and some truly exotic teas. But our signature drinks are our contemporary cocktails, many of them devised exclusively for us by leading mixologist, Grant Jarvis. Here are some of our most popular recipes. Each recipe makes one cocktail.

COCKTAIL EQUIPMENT:
- Boston shaker
- Hawthorn strainer
- Tea strainer
- Bar spoon (5ml)
- Muddler: either purpose-made, or a small pestle or rolling pin
- Set of cocktail measures, or small measuring jug with liquid quantities marked in 5ml gradations

GRANT'S SHAKING TIPS:
- The whole idea of shaking is to mix the ingredients, introduce water into the drink and super-chill your masterpiece.
- Fill the glass part of your Boston shaker slightly beyond the top with ice, place the metal section on squarely and push down firmly to seal.
- Always remember to shake with glass facing away from others to avoid accidents.
- Shake roughly to a quick ten count – no more, or the taste will be diluted.
- To break seal, tap with wrist on the joint.

YUMYUM'S MOJITO

Ideally you should start your preparations at least two days ahead: four days is even better but may test your patience to the limits. The aim is to introduce a subtle lemongrass flavour into your liquor, so take a bottle of Cuban white rum and pour out a shot. (This should, of course, be imbibed rather than tipped down the sink.) Bash two stalks of fresh lemongrass with a tenderiser or rolling pin, insert them into the bottle, replace cap, and leave to infuse for at least 48 hours.

EQUIPMENT: Muddler, bar spoon, straws
GLASSWARE: Highball tumbler
ICE: Crushed, either in a heavy-duty blender or wrapped in a linen cloth and bashed

- 1 lime, washed
- 7-8 leaves fresh mint, picked off the stalk
- 50ml lemongrass-infused Cuban white rum, or 25ml infused white and 25ml plain dark rums
- 3 bar spoons demerara or soft brown sugar

GARNISH:
- Extra sprigs of mint, Angostura bitters

1. Chop the lime into several chunks and place in tumbler.
2. Add the mint and sugar.
3. Muddle whilst counting to ten, or until the mint is bruised and you can see the fruit and herb juices collecting.
4. Fill tumbler with crushed ice and add the rum.
5. Stir well using the bar spoon.
6. Dip a straw into the liquid and use this to check taste upon your tongue.
7. Adjust if desired – more sugar can be added if the mix seems too sour.
8. Fill tumbler to top with more crushed ice.
9. Decorate with the extra mint and sprinkle 3-4 drops of Angostura on the top. Serve with two straws.

RED SNAPPER

EQUIPMENT: Boston shaker, hawthorn strainer, muddler
GLASSWARE: Martini cocktail glass
ICE: Whole ice cubes

- Half a long red chilli, deseeded if wished
- 4 basil leaves
- Black pepper
- Salt
- Balsamic vinegar
- Dash (5ml) freshly-squeezed lemon juice
- 40ml good quality tomato juice
- A few drops of Tabasco
- 50ml gin
- 10ml sirop de gomme

GARNISH:
- Slice of red chilli, cut lengthways; or a sliver of lemon zest carefully pushed through a basil leaf.

1. Place chilli and basil in the glass section of the shaker.
2. Add two grinds of the black pepper mill, a pinch of salt and a dash of balsamic vinegar.
3. Stir whilst you count to ten, then let the mixture rest for a few seconds.
4. Add the lemon juice, then the tomato juice and Tabasco.
5. Follow this with the gin and the sirop de gomme, and lastly fill up the shaker with the ice cubes.
6. Stir very gently: tomato juice appreciates reverential treatment and will separate in protest if shaken or stirred vigorously.
7. Strain into Martini glass using hawthorn strainer.
8. Decorate with the garnish you have chosen.

You can, if wished, place the glass on a saucer and surround the base with cucumber slices lightly sprinkled with sea salt.

BANGKOK BREAKFAST

EQUIPMENT: Boston shaker, hawthorn strainer, tea strainer
GLASSWARE: Martini cocktail glass well chilled in freezer
ICE: None

- 2 bar spoons clementine marmalade
- 50ml gin
- 20ml Grand Marnier
- 25ml freshly squeezed lemon juice

GARNISH:
- Slice of orange - optional

1. Spoon the marmalade into the glass section of the Boston shaker.
2. Add the gin, Grand Marnier and lemon juice.
3. Assemble the shaker and shake vigorously for 10 seconds.
4. Have your Martini glass ready.
5. Secure hawthorn strainer over metal section of shaker.
6. Holding shaker and strainer in one hand, take the tea strainer in the other and hold over the Martini glass.
7. Pour the cocktail through one strainer into the other.

HEAVY WEIGHT
venus and mars versions

EQUIPMENT: Muddler
GLASSWARE: Tumbler
ICE: Whole cubes

VENUS:
- 6 fresh raspberries
- 25ml dark rum
- 25ml Amaretto
- 25ml Chambord
- Optional: Champagne, Prosecco or Cava to top up glass

MARS:
- Follow recipe above, omitting both the feminine ingredients of raspberries and fizz!

1. Place 4 raspberries in tumbler and muddle until crushed.
2. Fill tumbler with ice cubes.
3. Pour rum over ice, followed by the Amaretto and the Chambord.
4. Stir gently to combine, and top up with fizz if desired.
5. Decorate with the remaining 2 raspberries.

SPRING SUMMER

non-alcoholic

EQUIPMENT: Boston shaker, hawthorn strainer
GLASSWARE: Highball tumbler
ICE: Whole cubes

- 1 heaped teaspoon fresh root ginger, peeled and chopped
- 5 chunks fresh watermelon, each about 4cm x 2cm x 2cm
- 10ml sirop de gomme
- 15ml freshly-squeezed lemon juice
- 20ml apple juice

GARNISH:
- Thin sliver of watermelon, rind retained

1. Place the ginger in the glass section of the shaker and muddle for ten seconds.
2. Add the watermelon chunks and continue muddling for a further twenty seconds.
3. Pour the remaining ingredients into the shaker, top up with ice and secure metal section.
4. Shake for 10 seconds.
5. Fill tumbler with ice cubes.
6. Strain cocktail through hawthorn strainer into tumbler.
7. Attach watermelon slice to rim of glass.

ABSTINENCE ON THE BEACH

non-alcoholic

GLASSWARE: Highball tumbler
ICE: Whole cubes

- 375ml mango juice
- 2 teaspoons natural yogurt
- 20ml vanilla syrup/sirop de vanille
- 3 ice cubes

Simplicity itself.
Place all the ingredients in a blender, blend for 15 seconds, and pour into your glass.

DIPPING SAUCES

SWEET CHILLI SAUCE

MAKES 300ML/24 TABLESPOONS:
- 150g long red chillies, deseeded if wished, and finely chopped in a processor
- 250ml water
- 450g caster sugar
- 250ml white vinegar
- 1 ½ tablespoons sea salt

Place the sugar, water and vinegar in a saucepan and bring to simmering point, then add the chillies and the salt. Simmer for ten minutes then turn off the heat, stir well, and leave to cool.

PEANUT SAUCE

MAKES 180ML:
(Sufficient for 4 people to accompany Sa-tay Chicken or King Prawns)
- 2 tablespoons vegetable oil
- 3 heaped teaspoons red curry paste
- 4 tablespoons dry-roasted peanuts, finely crushed
- 150ml coconut milk
- 1 tablespoon light soy sauce
- 1 tablespoon lemon juice

Heat the wok to medium and add the oil. After 20 seconds stir in the curry paste. Move around the wok for 10 seconds or so, until spitting, then add the peanuts. Cook for a further half minute until you can really smell the peanuts, then pour in the coconut milk and stir. When bubbling and starting to thicken, add the soy sauce and stir again. Remove from heat, mix in the lemon juice and leave to cool.

DIPPING SAUCES

CUCUMBER & CARROT RELISH

MAKES 250ML:
- 100ml rice vinegar
- 1 tablespoon caster sugar
- 1 teaspoon sea salt
- ¼ of a cucumber, sliced lengthways, seeds scooped out, then chopped
- ½ a medium carrot, peeled and finely chopped

Simply place all the ingredients in a plastic container, put the lid on securely, and shake vigorously for ten seconds. Leave for an hour before serving.

PLUM SAUCE

MAKES 250ML:
- 12 teaspoons mirabelle jam (eg St Dalfour Extra Jam)
- 4 teaspoons damson jam (eg Wilkin's Tiptree)
- 4 tablespoons rice vinegar

Place all the ingredients in a saucepan and heat very gently, stirring, until the jams have melted completely. Leave to cool.

WHERE TO FIND IT

Most ingredients are easily obtained from supermarkets and local shops, but a few are more difficult to locate. The list below is not exhaustive but should be of help to you in your quest

- **Fresh & Wild (FW)** Tel: 020 7254 2332
  32 Stoke Newington Church Street, N16.

- **Hoo Hing (HH)**
  Dorma Trading Park, Staffa Road, E10.
  Tel: 020 8988 6228
  Lockfield Avenue, Brimsdown, Enfield, EN3.
  Tel: 020 8344 9888
  Online/Home Delivery: www.hoohing.com

- **Loon Fung Supermarket (LF)**
  111 Brantwood Road, N15.
  Tel: 020 8365 1132
  42-44 Gerrard Street, Chinatown, W1.
  Tel: 020 7437 7332

- **London Starnight Video Supermarket (LS)**
  203-213 Mare Street, E8.
  Tel: 020 8985 2949

- **See Woo (SW)** Tel: 020 7439 8325
  18-20 Lisle Street, Chinatown, WC2.

- **Taste of Siam (TS)** Tel: 020 7383 5002
  47 Camden High Street, NW1.
  Tel: 020 7383 5002

- **Thai4UK (TF)** www.Thai4UK.com
  Online orders/home delivery
  Fresh produce direct from Thailand.
  3-4 days plus express service (not
  available on weekends or bank holidays).

Aubergines, pea & Thai: **LS, SW, TF, TS**
Basil, holy & sweet: **HH, LS, TF, TS**
Cassia Bark: **FW**
Chillies, orange (yellow): **TF**
Chinese Celery: **HH, LS**
Coriander Root: **LS, TF, TS**
Duck: boneless roast frozen: **HH, SW**
Duck Eggs, salted: **LF, LS, SW**
Galangal: **LS, SW, TF, TS**
Green Papaya: **LF, LS, SW, TF**
Green Peppercorns, fresh: **LF, LS, SW, TF, TS**
Kaffir Lime Leaves: **LS, SW, TF, TS**
Kra Chai: **SW, TF, TS**
Long Beans: **LS, SW, TF, TS**
Morning Glory: **LS, TF, TS**
Mushroom, various dried: **FW, LF, LS, SW, TS**
Mustard Greens: **LS, TF, VT**
Pandan Leaf: **LF, TF, SW**
Radish, Dried: **LF, LS, SW**
Shrimp, Dried: **SW**
Yellow Bean Soy: **LF**

ACKNOWLEDGMENTS

I would like to thank the following individuals and companies, without whom this book would never have been possible:

Everyone at YumYum, especially my beautiful wife Moy Choudhury, my management team Rithesh, Musthafa, Faz and Mannan; Runjit Garret and the fantastic teams in the kitchen and behind the bar.

Jaqi Clayton for her tireless work compiling and testing the recipes in this book.
Michelle Allmark, Paul West, Simon Nash, Michal Hicks, Adam Snow, Nina Sletten, Lorna Monk and Lindsay Kinniburgh at Ignite Marketing for their help and inspiration in producing and designing this book. Oz Dror for the marathon photography session.
Rouge for supplying the crockery and fabrics for the photo shoot.
Grant Jarvis our cocktail consultant for his huge contribution to both of our bars.
Nicky Johnson and Warren Smith for interior photography.

Thanks also to: Michael Beattie, Amanda Carrara, Chris Church, Gail & Stuart Coare, Erik de Graaff, Sue Heal, Andrew Hewson, Edna & Jack High, Luke Hudson, Bunchoo Iamdara, Rab MacWilliam, Michael Mulligan, Peter T. Scott, Susan & Andrew Sidell, Kartar Singh, Hana & Danny Sutton, Jack Uddin, Max Wallace, Rupert Wheeler. The crew at The Fishery, N16; Murat Poyraz and all at 101 Stoke Newington Church Street; Mike Strong & Justin Lee at North Walsham Fishmongers; Geoff Eastell of Eastell's Fruiterers, Paul Craske and team at Emery's Butchers, Martyn & Sam Hammond and colleagues at Head Cook & Bottlewasher, all in North Walsham, Norfolk. And to Alice Clayton.

This book is dedicated to my son Rishi.

Atique Choudhury

We would like to thank Rouge N16 for their kindness in providing many of the fabrics and ceramics used in the photo shoot for this book.

Rouge sell a wide range of gifts, handmade ceramics, fabrics, period and new furniture and decorative items, imported directly from China.

If you like what you have seen in this book why not pay a visit to their boutique store on Stoke Newington High Street where you can browse to your heart's content.

Rouge
158 Stoke Newington High Street
London
N16 7JL

Open 11am - 6.30pm, except Sun 12 noon - 5pm, closed Tues.
020 7275 0887

www.rouge-shop.co.uk